DRAMA CLASSICS

The Drama Classics series aims to offer the world's greatest plays in affordable paperback editions for students, actors and theatregoers. The hallmarks of the series are accessible introductions, uncluttered texts and an overall theatrical perspective.

Given that readers may be encountering a particular play for the first time, the introduction seeks to fill in the theatrical/ historical background and to outline the chief themes rather than concentrate on interpretational and textual analysis. Similarly the play-texts themselves are free of footnotes and other interpolations: instead there is an end-glossary of 'difficult' words and phrases.

The texts of the English-language plays in the series have been prepared taking full account of all existing scholarship. The foreign-language plays have been newly translated into a modern English that is both actable and accurate: many of the translators regularly have their work staged professionally.

Edited until his early death by Kenneth McLeish, the Drama Classics series continues with his aim of providing a first-class library of dramatic literature representing the best of world theatre.

Associate editors:
Professor Trevor R. Griffiths
Dr. Colin Counsell
School of Arts and Humanities
University of North London

DRAMA CLASSICS *the first hundred*

*The publishers welcome
suggestions for further titles*

DRAMA CLASSICS

WOYZECK

by
Georg Büchner

translated by
Gregory Motton

with an introduction by
Kenneth McLeish

NICK HERN BOOKS
London
www.nickhernbooks.co.uk

A Drama Classic

Woyzeck first published in Great Britain in this translation as a paperback original in 1996 by Nick Hern Books Limited, 14 Larden Road, London W3 7ST

Reprinted 1999, 2001, 2002, 2003, 2005

Copyright in the translation from the German © 1991, 1996 Gregory Motton

Copyright in the introduction © 1996 Nick Hern Books Ltd

Gregory Motton has asserted his moral right to be identified as the translator of this work

Typesetting by Country Setting, Kingsdown, Kent CT14 8ES
Printed by Bookmarque, Croydon, Surrey

A CIP catalogue record for this book is available from the British Library

ISBN 1 85459 183 5

Introduction

Georg Büchner (1813-1837)

Büchner came from a family of doctors and intended to follow
in their footsteps. Several documents survive from his schooldays: essays on such subjects as 'Friendship' and 'Suicide', and
the formal speeches that selected pupils were expected to give
on public occasions. They show that as a teenager he already
had an original turn of mind and, in the way he put over his
arguments, the knack for rhetoric one might perhaps expect
from a future playwright.

There is nothing in this schoolwork to suggest interest in any
of the arts, much less drama, and although when Büchner
went to university in Strasbourg at the age of eighteen he
abandoned his vocation for medicine, his alternative ambitions
were not literary but directed towards philosophy and
academic research. Officially, research won. He specialised
in natural science (zoology and anatomy), and made rapid
progress up the academic ladder, winning a doctorate with
a dissertation on the nervous system of the barbel at 22 and
being appointed lecturer in anatomy at Zürich University a
year after that.

None of this was much different from the career of most very
bright students of the day. However, almost from the start of

his university career, Büchner's main passion was not for work but for politics. He began with student debates and discussions, then (during a year 'out' at Giessen University) joined the radical movement known as 'Young Germany', co-founded the grandly-named Secret Society for the Rights of Man, and was one of the authors of a pamphlet (*The Hessian Courier*) which urged working people of Hesse, his native part of Germany, to win social rights by force. His co-authors of this document were arrested and imprisoned. Büchner escaped by denying any involvement with the pamphlet, by accepting house-arrest at his parents' home, and then by slipping out of Germany forever, first back to Strasbourg and his fiancée Minna Jaeglé, and then to his lectureship in Zürich.

Despite the revolutionary fervour of his politics, Büchner seems to have been a timid man, backing down in the face of parental disapproval of his activism and seldom venturing out to meet the 'ordinary people' whose rights he so vociferously championed. This timidity may have been aggravated by ill-health. From childhood he was prone to migraine and stomach disorders; he suffered a serious attack of meningitis when he was 20; and in February 1837, just as his adult career was beginning, he contracted typhus and died.

It is to Büchner's combination of radical fervour and physical timidity that we owe his plays. In five desperate weeks in 1835, penniless and on the run from the secret police, he wrote *Danton's Death*: a play about the despair and disillusion felt by Danton, the French Revolutionary leader whose colleagues turned on him, rejected his ideals and condemned him to the guillotine. In 1836, when he was under house-arrest, he wrote (for a prize competition) *Leonce and Lena*, about a prince and princess who decide to rescue their country from aristocratic corruption and make it an ideal state. *Woyzeck*, uncompleted at his death, is about an ordinary man who murders his mistress. It is impossible to say what direction Büchner would have taken had he survived and seen any of these works performed – they reached the stage three generations after his death. But he might be surprised to find that, nowadays, he is remembered as a dramatist. His passion and drive were less for theatre than for his political and social ideas, and he seems to have chosen the form of drama chiefly for convenience – it was quicker to write a play than a novel or a work of political philosophy. He was a playwright by default rather than by conviction.

Woyzeck: **What Happens in the Play**

In a series of short scenes, Büchner shows us the case-history of Franz Woyzeck, a lowly soldier. Woyzeck is not bright, but is intelligent enough to know that he is being stifled by his own life. It offers him no self-esteem, no appreciation from others, no escape from the daily grind for survival or the poverty and hopelessness of his situation. We see him gathering sticks with a fellow-soldier, Andres, drinking in an inn, shaving his Captain (who mocks him mercilessly), standing like an organ-grinder's monkey while the regiment's Doctor, an upper-class buffoon, makes him perform such tricks as wiggling his ears to amuse the medical students. He has hallucinations, sees apparitions and feels that he is going mad. There is only one source of warmth in his life: his lover Marie and their innocent young son. But Marie is unfaithful, and Woyzeck's drinking-companions tell him that she is having sex with the regiment's brainless but handsome Drum Major, whom she and Woyzeck have earlier encountered at a fair. Woyzeck fights the Drum Major and loses. He contemplates suicide; he buys a knife. But he arranges first to meet Marie in a wood by a pond, and her coldness finally drives him over the edge; and he murders her. The play as we have it – not necessarily as Büchner planned it – concludes with Woyzeck appearing at the inn, covered in blood, and then returning to the lake and wading out into the water to throw away the knife, deeper and deeper until the action ends.

The Political Background

Büchner was born a generation after the French Revolution and a couple of years before the squabbling and mutually suspicious countries of Europe, with enormous effort, achieved enough military and political unity to defeat Napoleon and end his vision of a single, French-dominated, European empire. The shockwaves from these two events produced a kind of political paralysis throughout the continent and put an abrupt end to all the experiments with liberalism, expansion of democracy, extension of human rights and religious tolerance which had marked the last decades of the eighteenth century. At a stroke, political and social radicalism, of the kind advocated by such thinkers as Thomas Paine (whose *The Rights of Man* and *The Age of Reason* had inspired revolutionaries everywhere, from France to South and North America), became suspect if not treasonable in the eyes of the authorities, and highly dangerous for those who preached it.

Reactions to this kind of thinking varied according to the self-image and stability of each European state. Britain, for example, treated radical thinkers as not so much dangerous as eccentric, whether they were prison reformers such as Elizabeth Fry, anti-slavery campaigners such as William Wilberforce, hot-headed libertarians such as Percy Bysshe Shelley or social reformers such as Robert Owen. Other states, by contrast, reacted with paranoia. In Vienna in the 1810s and 1820s, a surface of self-satisfied, bourgeois bumble masked strict political control, a system administered by secret police and touching the lives of even such amiable innocents as Franz Schubert and his circle of poets and musicians. In smaller states, such as the many shakily-governed German princedoms, oppression was harsh, unconcealed and ruthlessly devoted to retaining the wealth and power of the ruling family and its aristocratic hangers-on. In the 1820s the Karlsbad Decrees (outlawing the publication, in books, pamphlets or speeches, of anti-authoritarian views) led to a political witchhunt and the disappearance and death of thousands of over-voluble intellectuals and the people who bought their writings or went to hear them speak.

Hesse-Darmstadt, Büchner's home state, is a striking example of the kind of feudal tyranny which such measures were intended to maintain. In 1830, when Grand-Duke Ludwig II succeeded to the throne, there were some three-quarters of a million inhabitants arranged in a pyramid of authority in which people from each level were responsible to, and utterly in the power of, those on the level above. The annual tax revenue was some six million gulden – and in the year when Ludwig succeeded, he imposed an arbitrary, additional tax of two million gulden, to pay debts he had incurred as Prince in Waiting. The peasants revolted, the rebellion was bloodily crushed, and a constitution which Ludwig's predecessor had created in 1820 (a kind of *Magna Carta* granting limited legal and political rights) was cancelled. Hesse reverted to its former medieval political condition, that of an authoritarian, ultra-conservative autocracy.

In such a situation, it was hardly surprising that students – even including young men like Büchner, whose father was directly in the service of Grand-Duke Ludwig – should feast on the forbidden fruits of political philosophy and dissent. Evidence suggests that the authorities tolerated university discussion groups and even allowed the students to form 'secret' political societies (whose meetings they nevertheless infiltrated with spies who kept detailed minutes). But as soon as there was any threat that the hot air of such gatherings might be replaced by practical activity, that passionate speeches to half a dozen friends might give way to public agitation, they pounced. This is the atmosphere in which Büchner co-wrote and disseminated his pamphlet, *The Hessian Courier*, in 1834. The document is a mixture of statistics (on who in Hesse paid tax and who benefited from it – the Grand-Ducal household alone costing nearly one million gulden a year), wild generalisations about the nature of freedom and the human soul, and a final prophecy that if people organised themselves, all corrupt rulers would be swept away and Germany would be united as a single, Christian, democratic Utopia.

The authors of *The Hessian Courier* held a view characteristic of many intellectual revolutionaries: that the case they presented was so compelling that no one would resist it, that it only had to be stated for the scales to fall from everyone's eyes and the good times roll for all. (It was typical of their naivety that they circulated the pamphlet among farmers and fieldworkers, not realising that few were literate or sufficiently learned in philosophy or rhetoric to follow its arguments.) When they were arrested, they reacted with a kind of self-regarding, panicky despair which contrasted sharply with the rigour and vehemence of their earlier polemic. Weidig, Büchner's main co-author, collapsed under interrogation (not torture) and later committed suicide in prison, and Büchner escaped punishment by grovelling to the authorities and to his family (promising to avoid all politics in future), and threw himself into work for his doctorate on the one hand, and into furiously polemical playwriting on the other.

The Real Woyzeck

Woyzeck is based on a real case-history, a murder and controversial trial of the early 1820s, which Büchner probably read about in medical journals from his father's library. In 1821, in Leipzig, Johann Christian Woyzeck was arrested for stabbing to death his lover, Frau Woost. He was tried and sentenced to death in 1822. But before the execution, he told a visiting clergyman that he had seen visions and heard voices telling him to commit the murder, and his defence lawyers lodged an appeal so that his mental state could be thoroughly examined. The examining physician, Dr J.C.A. Clarus, pronounced Woyzeck sane, and the unfortunate man was executed in 1824. But other specialists disputed the examination findings, and Clarus was so incensed that he published a self-justifying account in a medical journal (the one Büchner probably read). The controversy rumbled on for another decade, to be resolved only when a fresh enquiry confirmed Woyzeck's sanity and vindicated Clarus in 1838.

Johann Christian Woyzeck was born in 1780, orphaned in 1783, and passed the rest of his life drifting from place to place throughout Germany and Austria. He spent some time as a tramp, took odd jobs as farmhand or waiter, and tried to find status and legitimate employment by enlisting as a soldier in any army that would have him, from the Royal Swedish Infantry to the private regiment of the Duke of Mecklenburg. Illiterate and possibly simple-minded, he was incapable of keeping any position for long, and gradually lost all feelings of self-worth. Eventually, in Leipzig, he eked out an existence as a barber, and formed a relationship with his landlady Frau Woost, a widow. Two years later, Woyzeck discovered that Woost had a weakness for soldiers and was cuckolding him. He bought a knife and stabbed her dead.

During Clarus' examinations, Woyzeck seems to have broken down – not so much mentally as spiritually. He ranted about the poverty and injustice of his life, his 'Devil-inspired' appetites for drink and sex, the way the whole world despised him, the conspiracies against him of everyone from innkeepers to army sergeants, from women to freemasons – and he claimed that giant mushrooms had appeared out of nowhere to threaten him, and that voices from the sky or from under the ground had told him to 'Stick the Woost dead'. His gaolers reported that when he was alone he babbled to himself, to God, to the walls and ceiling of his cell. Despite all this, Clarus decided that although Woyzeck was degenerate and pitiable, a human being wrecked by 'idleness, gambling, drink, sex and bad company', he was mentally enough in control to know what he was doing and was therefore guilty as charged.

When Büchner made his play from this material, he kept many of the details – indeed, used several words and phrases from the original documents – but completely changed the perspective. He made Woyzeck not an isolated, individual case-study but an emblem of down-trodden, despairing humanity, his dignity and self-esteem eroded by circumstances and the assaults of his 'superiors' in rank and class. He turned Clarus – in real life a pompous but honest ass – into a middle-class buffoon and charlatan, and to increase this impression added details from his own observations. One of his anatomy lecturers had a party trick to show each new intake of students: he brought his young son into the lecture-room and made the boy demonstrate the muscles of the face by wiggling his ears (see page 34). Another (the distinguished scientist Justus Liebig) paid soldiers to eat nothing but peas, so that he could conduct experiments on how this diet affected their urine (see page 21). As with Woyzeck's terror of mushrooms (a phobia familiar to all psychiatrists) and of the secretive, middle- and upper-class freemasons, who were thought by ordinary people to be alchemists and devil-worshippers, fact in these instances was as extraordinary as anything fiction could invent.

Woyzeck

In January 1837, Büchner wrote from Switzerland to his fiancée Minna Jaeglé that he had two plays all but ready for publication. He neither named them nor described them, and when he died six weeks later one of the plays had disappeared entirely and the other survived only as a heap of manuscript papers. Scholars suggest that Jaeglé, a pastor's daughter, disapproved of Büchner's dramatic works, either because of their politics or because of the coarseness of their language. They say that after the papers were returned to her, she may have destroyed one of the plays (*Pietro Aretino*) altogether, and left the other (*Woyzeck*) only because the manuscript looked indecipherable. It was not till 1879 that *Woyzeck* was finally published, not till 1913 that it was first performed, and not till 1967 that the first 'definitive' edition of the text was made. (On the problems of working out Büchner's precise intentions, see page xxi.)

This long-drawn-out struggle for existence means that *Woyzeck* is a play which belongs to two dramatic eras at once. The thought behind it was original and revolutionary for its age, but that age was firmly the first half of the nineteenth century. However, the play was published and first performed right at the heart of all the social, political, psychological, literary and dramatic experiments which marked the end of the nineteenth century and the first decades of the twentieth, and it influenced *avant-garde* work of all kinds at one of the most anarchic and creative periods in the history of the arts in Europe. For three-quarters of a century it had lain like a time-bomb, unknown but ticking until the time was right for it to explode – and after it burst on the scene, with the stunning but 80-years-delayed Munich première in 1913, the artistic world was never the same again. It was as if it had been written not sixty years before but yesterday, as if its author were a contemporary not of Schiller and Beethoven but of such experimental, twentieth-century innovators as Picasso, Stravinsky and D.W. Griffith. In particular, it was a crucial influence on that seminal artistic movement of the late nineteenth and early twentieth centuries, Expressionism, devoted to showing the psychological intensity and emotional states which underlie even the simplest words and actions. *Woyzeck*'s bleak, uncompromising power, achieved by the simplest of means, allies it to a body of Expressionist work of every conceivable kind: the plays and diaries of August Strindberg, the paintings of Edvard Munch (eg *The Scream*), the poems of Rainer Maria Rilke, the music of Arnold Schönberg and his pupil Alban Berg (whose 1925 opera *Wozzeck* sets Büchner's text word for word) and the novels of André Maurois in France and the young Hermann Hesse in Germany. Kafka read it in the 1920s, and its effects can be seen in stories and novels, though he added a streak of desperate, surreal humour only hinted at by Büchner. In the 1920s, the film director Friedrich Murnau worked on a stage version of *Woyzeck*, and was so impressed by its stifling psychological atmosphere that he looked for a way to reproduce on film what he called its feeling of 'overwhelming doom' – and, in *Nosferatu* (1922), made the first-ever horror film.

Form of the Play

If one considers *Woyzeck* in terms of the drama of its own day, indeed of all Western theatre that had gone before the 1830s, it was unique. Since ancient Greek times, all tragedies had followed the same broad patterns of form and content. In form, they were constructed as narratives, events following one another in a sequence organised like a journey. Each scene developed out of those which preceded it and led into those which followed it. The links might not be obvious or smooth, but they were there. *Woyzeck*, by contrast, is like a jigsaw, gradually built up before our eyes. Each of its twenty-four scenes is self-contained. None flows out of or into any of the others. Our picture of each character, and of the developing situation, does not grow organically, like a plant (as happens in earlier drama). Rather, it is a kind of collage, in which each new piece changes the total picture, by juxtaposition rather than development. This method became standard in the arts of the twentieth century – examples are film *montage*, 'block construction' in classical music, 'epic theatre' in drama, cubism in painting – but in 1836 it was unprecedented.

There are two possible reasons for this unusual form. One is Büchner's probable working-method as he wrote the play. Unlike his earlier plays, which he dashed off in sustained creative bursts, he seems to have scribbled the scenes of *Woyzeck* randomly, like notes or diary entries, as ideas occurred to him. Some were complete, others fragments of themes or scraps of dialogue. Possibly he intended, at a later stage, to edit them into the coherent and consecutive Acts which were standard in plays of his time – and death prevented him. But the second reason is equally plausible: that the *montage* form was deliberate, and that the play was never intended to be conventional. Büchner's main 'literary' activities, outside drama, were the arguing of political points of view and the preparation and presentation of scientific research. In pamphlets, essays and political speeches, from his schooldays onwards, he showed a fine grasp of the rhetorical methods used by ancient Greek philosophers and Roman orators. The whole argument is divided into topics or 'points', each of which is delivered as a self-contained unit before the speaker or writer moves on to the next. (The method is still used in law-court oratory today.) Similarly, a scientific presentation is a collection of self-contained expositions or demonstrations, strung on a thread like beads on a string, each making its point in its own individual way. This is how *Woyzeck* is constructed. Individually, the scenes can seem trivial or meaningless: their power comes only when the play is taken as a whole. Büchner created a different structure for each of his surviving plays, according to the nature of his material. *Danton's Death* used original letters, speeches and other documents in a way learned from Shakespeare's or Schiller's treatment of literary sources in such plays as *Julius Caesar* or *Mary Stuart*. *Leonce and Lena* was like a Grimm Brothers fairy story, dramatised. The original material of *Woyzeck* was a medical case-study, and it conformed to the presentational methods of science and not of art.

Tragic Heroes and Dramatic Meaning

Woyzeck's second uniqueness, in terms of the drama of its time, was in its content. Until then, almost by definition, European tragedy had centred on the dilemmas and suffering of 'great' people. Only grandees, it was felt, had sufficient position and moral stature to symbolise suffering humanity as a whole. As Aristotle put it, only the fall of a 'great' person – a fall resulting from an endemic 'tragic flaw' – was able to evoke the 'pity and terror' which tragedy, in order to be effective, needed to encourage in its audience. Dignity and aspiration were assumed to belong only to the demigods and heroes of Greek plays or the monarchs and nobles of Renaissance and post-Renaissance drama. Ordinary people made excellent characters for comedy, but if they appeared at all in tragedy it was in such cameo roles as servants, soldiers, entertainers or the unwashed (and usually unruly) mob.

Towards the end of the eighteenth century, this situation began to change. Playwrights such as Schiller, writing tragedies based on historical events, began to experiment with heroes and heroines who were not aristocrats. In the 1590s, when Shakespeare dramatised the story of Joan of Arc, it was as a subplot in *Henry VI*, his huge tapestry of the Wars of the Roses. Schiller's *The Maid of Orleans* (1801), by contrast, puts her at the heart of the action. Schiller also wrote a play, *William Tell* (1804), centred on an ordinary man who became a Swiss revolutionary leader. The hero of Büchner's own *Danton's Death* (1835) is not a prince but a lawyer-politician. None the less, even heroes like these, by reason of their deeds, are extra-ordinary rather than everyday, and their plights could be dramatised to illustrate general themes in the same way as the gods and monarchs of traditional tragedy. In the early decades of the nineteenth century, novelists such as Victor Hugo and Charles Dickens began to make tragedy from the stories of ordinary people, asserting for the first time the possibility of dignity and moral 'greatness' in a kind of person still dismissed by middle- and upper-class society at large. But *Woyzeck* was the first stage drama ever to make tragedy from the plight of someone with no social standing or claim whatever.

Such an imaginative leap was hardly large in terms of Büchner's politics, but artistically it was astounding, and it remained without parallel for almost the rest of the century. (Tragedy became resolutely middle-class, as in the plays of Ibsen. 'Ordinary' people's dilemmas were the province, on stage, of melodrama, either ephemeral blood-and-thunder or the more 'elevated' work of such writers as Dion Boucicault, whose 'working-class tragedies' are melodramas in all but name.) The simple part of Büchner's enterprise was to turn all the stereotypes on their heads. In *Woyzeck* the higher a character's class, the more negligible that character becomes; the lower the class, the more sympathetic the character. The Captain and Doctor are two-dimensional, caricatures respec-tively of casual sadism and insane experiment. At the next level down of society, the Drum Major and Journeymen are opinionated and dangerous. Only the people at the bottom of the social heap – Woyzeck himself, Andres, Marie, Margret, the Grandmother – are presented with depth and sympathy.

In the earlier world of Aristotelian tragedy, the hero is a person of high dignity, who challenges fate and loses everything. In Büchner's world, Woyzeck has the dignity not of high rank or reputation, but which belongs to all human souls, and his tragedy is that he is unable to see it, is blind to his own worth and relies instead on something outside himself, his relationship with Marie. It is when the world tramples on that, as on everything else in his life, that he is tipped into despair and irrevocable action. None the less, Büchner's view of the remorselessness of fate is little different from, say, Sophocles' in *King Oedipus* or Shakespeare's in *Othello*. The chief difference between Woyzeck and earlier tragic heroes is that he has had no choice whatever in his situation. Whereas their dilemmas are partly self-induced, he is trapped by what he is and by other people's actions and reactions. But once the trap is sprung, there is no difference between him and them, either in tragic status, moral dignity or the pity and terror they evoke in us. If one looks for moral messages in tragedy – as Aristotle, for one, insisted we should – they are as easy to find in *Woyzeck* as in any of the plays which preceded it.

Naturalism and Expressionism

For all *Woyzeck's* philosophical and tragic resonance, Büchner eschews grandeur: his play is entirely naturalistic in style and tone. The scenes are as short as fragments of real conversation or dreams, and the language is clipped and ordinary, with 'literary' and rhetorical turns of phrase reserved for the self-important (the Captain, the Doctor) or the drunk (the Journeyman who preaches a mock sermon). Woyzeck changes the way he talks depending on who is with him – he is submissive with superiors, affectionate or desperate with Marie, full of bravado with the drinkers in the inn, colloquial with Andres, and fragmentary and disturbed when he is alone, talking to himself. He and the other 'ordinary' characters speak dialect, with the result that the 'standard' speech used by the Captain and Doctor seems bizarre and unreal. The play is full of (genuine) Hessian folk-songs, occasionally complete but more often in fragments and snatches, and Büchner uses them (as in real life) to reveal the thoughts and emotions in each singer's mind.

This ability of *Woyzeck* to reveal its characters' inner turmoil was one of the main reasons for its enormous influence almost as soon as it was rediscovered and performed in the early twentieth century (see page xiv), one of the most sensational cases of posthumous discovery in the whole of modern literature. The ground had been prepared by such nineteenth-century works as Wagner's music-dramas and the novels of Zola and Dostoevsky, not to mention the rise of Freud and Freudian analysis in the 1900s, but until *Woyzeck* showed the way, artists, and playwrights in particular, had problems finding suitable forms and shapes to articulate the new ideas. *Woyzeck*'s stage history is sparse: it is challenging to stage and has had surprisingly few major productions for a work of such importance (most notably two by the Berlin Ensemble and one directed by Ingmar Bergman). But no other work has had such an extraordinary influence on 'experimental' twentieth-century drama of all kinds. The list of writers whose work would have been utterly different if it had not existed includes Alfred Jarry and Frank Wedekind at the start of the century, Antoine Artaud in the 1930s, Bertolt Brecht in the 1930s-40s, Ingmar Bergman in the 1950s, Samuel Beckett, Friedrich Dürrenmatt and Peter Weiss.

Büchner's Text

When Büchner died, he left four bundles of papers concerned with *Woyzeck*. Three contained jottings and drafts of individual scenes, the fourth a copy of the play as we have it, up to the scene where Woyzeck gives Andres his possessions (page 40). Most scholars assume that this last version was a fair copy, and that when Büchner told his fiancée that 'a week's work' was needed to finish the play, he meant copying out the last few scenes and checking the whole thing. (Where a scene existed complete in the other versions, for example the fairground scene, page 9, Büchner merely indicated its presence in this document, leaving a blank page to copy it down on later.)

If the long manuscript *was* a fair copy, then it shows Büchner's very last thoughts on the play, and the version we have must be reasonably close to his intentions. Unfortunately, his handwriting was so bad that when his brother assembled his manuscripts for publication in 1850, he found it impossible to read *Woyzeck* and left it out of the edition. The next editor, K.E. Franzos, who published the play in 1879, 43 years after it was written, did his best to untangle the *Woyzeck* papers, but created almost as many problems as he solved. He made simple mistakes in deciphering Büchner's writing, for example misreading the play's title as *Wozzeck* and the character-name Karl as 'Fool' (German *Narr*). More seriously, he juggled the order of scenes to make what he thought was 'more dramatic sense', and to help the handwriting stand out more clearly he washed the papers with a mixture of ammonia and distilled water, which worked for a time but then darkened the pages and made them even more illegible. It was not till the manuscript was photographically treated in the 1940s (using wartime techniques for deciphering secret documents) that a more correct text was made, and the definitive scholarly edition was not published until 1967.

For the ordinary reader or performer, the most important matter arising from all this is the order of scenes. The 'definitive' order, first established by Werner R. Lehman in 1967 and followed in this translation, is:

1. Woyzeck and Andres cut wood
2. Marie and Margret watch the parade
3. Fairground scene
4. In the tent
5. Marie's room: the 'earrings scene'
6. Woyzeck shaves the Captain
7. Marie and the Drum Major
8. Woyzeck confronts Marie
9. Woyzeck and the Doctor: the 'peeing on the wall' scene
10. The Captain and Doctor humiliate Woyzeck
11. The guardroom: Woyzeck says he must go to the dance
12. First inn scene: Woyzeck says Marie and the Drum Major dancing
13. Woyzeck hallucinates in a field
14. Woyzeck tries to tell Andres about his 'voices'
15*. The Doctor lectures to his students
16. Woyzeck and the Drum Major fight
17*. Woyzeck tells Andres of his dream of buying a knife

[*Scenes 15 and 17 are not in Büchner's final draft, but are supplied from earlier manuscripts.]

This order failed to convince the play's earlier editors and translators. Failing to understand Büchner's *montage* system of construction, they tried to make the play conform to earlier notions of dramatic narrative, and re-ordered the scenes accordingly. In particular, they wanted to begin not by plunging straight into the action but with scenes which set out the situation and characters as clearly as possible. For this purpose, they began with Scene 6 (Woyzeck shaving the Captain) and then Scene 9 (Woyzeck and the Doctor), relegating until later in the play the scene where Woyzeck and Andres cut wood (Scene 1). Other editors jumbled the scene-order even further. Franzos' 1879 edition, for example, runs 6, 3, 9, 5, 15, 1, 2, 4, 7, 10, 8, 16, 11, 12, 13, 14, 17, 16, 21, 20, 22, 23, 24, fragment 1, fragment 4 (on fragments, see below), and G. Witkowski's 1920 edition, though in many ways close to the later 'definitive' version, omits several scenes entirely (dismissing them as 'sketches'), and changes the meaning of the play by altering the ending. Witkowski's order is 10, 1, 2, 3, 4, 6, 7, 11, 12, 13, 14, 8, 9, 16, 18, 19, 20, 15, fragment 1. Such choices are strange only if we believe that Büchner's final manuscript was a fair copy; if not, then it is anyone's guess as to which order would have been Büchner's final choice. Indeed, had he lived he might have gone on working on the play, giving it a different shape entirely.

There are also several fragments, too short or too puzzling to have found secure places in the main text. (They are printed here in the appendix, page 49.) Fragment 1 shows us Woyzeck, his young son Christian and the Idiot Karl. It is often inserted in the play after the scene where Woyzeck sees Marie dancing with the Drum Major (Scene 12), or after the fragment in which the children discuss the body (that is, after Scene 22 or Scene 23). Fragment 2 shows two men (possibly the Journeymen from earlier in the play) in the woods, hearing 'the water calling' and reflecting that 'no one's been drowned for a long time here'. This is often inserted after the murder scene (Scene 22), after the second inn scene (Scene 23), or, more controversially, at the very end of the play (after Scene 24). In Fragment 3, children talk excitedly of a body by the pond, and rush off to see it. This is often inserted after the murder scene (Scene 22), or with Fragment 2 after the second inn scene (Scene 23). Fragment 4, the last and most enigmatic, is a single speech by a Coroner talking of a 'decent murder, a real murder', and so on. No one knows where this was meant to fit in the text as we have it. Some make it a self-contained insert after the second inn-scene (Scene 23), others think that it is all that survives of a trial- or execution-scene which Büchner never finished, either because of his death or because the play seemed to him complete as it stood, the existing conclusion rounding off the action and meaning of the tragedy more convincingly than any other.

Kenneth McLeish, 1996

For Further Reading

Good introductions to both Büchner's life and his work are A.H.J. Knight, *Georg Büchner* (revised edition 1972; out of date on the manuscripts but good on Büchner's life and with ample quotations – alas, only in German – from relevant documents) and Julian Hilton, *Georg Büchner* (1982). Maurice Benn, *The Drama of Revolt* (1976) is a critical study of all Büchner's writing, heavyweight but meaty. Readers with access to a university library, and a particular interest in political thought in 1830s Germany, are directed to Dorothy James' article 'The "Interesting Case" of Büchner's *Woyzeck*' in *Patterns of Change: Essays in Honour of Ronald Peacock* (ed D. James and S. Ranawake, New York 1990). We also recommend the Introductions and other editorial material in Michael Patterson's 1987 Methuen edition of Büchner's complete plays, one of the most accessible of all English-language assessments of his work.

Georg Büchner: Key Dates

1813   Born, 17 October

1825   At school in Darmstadt

1831   At university in Strasbourg

1833   Compulsory (and unwelcome) year 'out', studying at
         University of Giessen; forms student political societies

1834   Begins active political work; co-writes *The Hessian
         Courier*; denounced and condemned to house-arrest in
         Darmstadt; works for his doctorate

1835   *Danton's Death* written (in five weeks in January and
         February); flees secret police and goes into exile in
         Strasbourg; translates Hugo's plays *Lucretia Borgia* and
         Mary Tudor; writes long short story *Lenz*, about a
         writer who goes insane

1836   (Summer) writes *Leonce and Lena* to enter for a prize,
         but submits it too late; (September) awarded doctorate
         by University of Zürich; (October) moves to Zürich to
         take up post as lecturer in anatomy at the University;
         works on *Pietro Aretino* and *Woyzeck*

1837   (January) writes to his fiancée that one play
         (presumably *Pietro Aretino* – there is no evidence and

the play is lost) is ready for publication and that it will take 'a week's work' to finish another (presumably *Woyzeck*); (February) contracts typhus and dies (on the 19th, after a three-week illness)

WOYZECK

Acknowledgement

Sincere thanks to Ben Hopkins for checking my translation and pointing out errors.   G.M

Characters

in order of appearance

Woyzeck, *a soldier*

Andres, *a soldier*

Marie, *Woyzeck's lover*

Margret, *her neighbour*

Captain

Old Man with hurdy-gurdy

Barker in the fairground

Sergeant

Drum Major

Showman

Doctor

Two Journeymen

Drinkers

Jew

Idiot (Karl)

Grandmother

Käthe, *a tavern girl*

Girls

Others:

Woyzeck's and Marie's Child (Christian)

Other children

Medical students

Barker's wife

Performing monkey

Performing horse

Townspeople

Soldiers

Notes

The Captain and Doctor are commissioned officers, of a higher social class than any other characters. The Drum Major is a non-commissioned officer, chosen for dazzle and swagger; his sole duty is to lead the regiment in parades and marches. The journeymen are apprentices who have served their time and are, so to speak, junior craftsmen, one rung below 'masters'.

1.

Open fields, the town in the distance.

WOYZECK *and* ANDRES *splitting wood.* ANDRES *whistles.*

WOYZECK. Yes, Andres, the place is cursed. See that patch of light over there where the mushrooms are growing? That's where the head rolls in the evenings. Someone picked it up once, he thought it was a hedgehog. Three days and three nights and then he was in his coffin. (*Quietly.*) It was the freemasons, I'm sure of it, freemasons. Ssh!

ANDRES.   Two hares sitting there
            Eating the grass
            Until it was bare –

WOYZECK. Ssh! Do you hear, Andres, do you hear? Something's moving

ANDRES.   Eating up the tiny shoots,
            Eating the grass
            Down to the roots –

WOYZECK. Something's behind me, beneath me.

He stamps on the ground.

Hollow, d'you hear? Completely hollow under there. Freemasons.

ANDRES. I'm scared.

WOYZECK. Strange how quiet it is. You want to hold your
    breath. Andres?

ANDRES. What?

WOYZECK. Say something.

He stares ahead.

Andres, it's so bright! The town is glowing. There's fire
travelling across the sky, and down here the din of trumpets.
How it draws you in. Quick, don't look behind you.

He drags him into the bushes.

ANDRES (*after a pause*). Woyzeck, do you still hear it?

WOYZECK. Silent, completely silent. As if the world was
    dead.

ANDRES. What was that? The drum's going. We'd better go.

2.

In town.

MARIE *with her* CHILD *at the window.* [MARGRET.] *The retreat passes, led by the* DRUM MAJOR.

MARIE (*rocking the child on her arm*). Bum, bum, bum. Hear that? They're coming.

MARGRET. What a man, like a tree.

MARIE. He stands on his feet like a lion.

[*The* DRUM MAJOR *salutes.*]

MARGRET. Giving him the eye, eh? Neighbour, it's not like you.

MARIE. So what? You can take your eyes to the Jew and get them polished and sell them for a couple of buttons.

MARGRET. What? You? You? Little miss virgin? I'm an honest woman, me, but we all know you can see right through a pair of leather trousers.

[*She goes.*]

MARIE. Slut!

She shuts the window.

Come on, my own boy, let people talk. You're only the poor son of a whore but you're still my pride and joy with your shameless face. There, there . . .

What will you do with your eyes that are wild?
What will you do with your fatherless child?
There's nothing to do

But sit here and sing.
Rockabye, rockabye, poor little thing,
There's nothing for you . . .

A knock on the window.

Who's that? Is that you, Franz? Come in.

WOYZECK. I can't. Got to muster.

MARIE. Been cutting wood for the Captain?

WOYZECK. Yes, Marie.

MARIE. What's wrong, Franz? You look destroyed.

WOYZECK (*secretively*). Things have been happening again,
Marie, lots of things. Isn't it written – 'and there was smoke
coming from the land as from an oven. . .'

MARIE. Franz!

WOYZECK. It followed me all the way to the edge of town.
Something we don't understand, something that will drive
us out of our minds. What will become of it?

MARIE. Franz!

WOYZECK. I've got to go. At the fair tonight, then. I've put
aside a bit again.

He goes.

MARIE. What a man. He's possessed. He didn't even look at
his child. He'll go mad with thinking. What are you so quiet
for, boy? Are you scared? It's getting dark, you could think
you were blind. Nothing but the streetlamp shining in. I
can't bear it, I'm shaking.

She goes out.

3.

The fair. Lights, people.

An OLD MAN *sings while a* CHILD *dances to a hurdy-gurdy.*

OLD MAN.   On earth we can't abide,
            We all must die
            As everybody knows –

    [WOYZECK *and* MARIE *come in.*]

WOYZECK. Hey-hup, poor old man. Poor child, little child, sorrows and joys.

MARIE. When the fools talk sense then they fool us all. What a funny world, a beautiful world.

    They move on to the BARKER. *He is in front of a stall with his wife in trousers and a monkey dressed in a suit.*

BARKER. Gentlemen! Gentlemen! Observe this creature God has created. A nothing, a mere nothing at all. But see what he has achieved; he walks upright, has a coat and trousers, carries a sword. The monkey is a soldier. Though that's not saying much, the lowest form of humanity. Now, bow to us, that's it, now you're a baron, give us a kiss.

    He plays a trumpet.

    The little blighter is musical. Gentlemen, here you see the astronomical horse and little canaries favoured by all the crowned heads of Europe. Tell you everything, how old, how many children, what illnesses. The performance will now begin. The commencement of the commencement.

WOYZECK. You want a go?

MARIE. Don't mind if I do. It must be nice in there. Look at the tassels the man has, and his wife's got trousers.

They go inside the tent. The DRUM MAJOR *and* SERGEANT *come in.*

DRUM MAJOR. Hold it. Did you see her? What a woman.

SERGEANT. By the devil, you could foal a cavalry regiment out of her.

DRUM MAJOR. And breed Drum Majors.

SERGEANT. Look at the way she holds her head. You'd think the weight of all that black hair would drag her down. And her eyes . . .

DRUM MAJOR. Like looking down a well. Or a chimney. Quick, after her.

4.

Inside the tent.

[MARIE, WOYZECK, DRUM MAJOR, SERGEANT.]

MARIE. What lights.

WOYZECK. Yes, Marie, black cats with fiery eyes. Oh, what
an evening.

The SHOWMAN *leads in a horse.*

SHOWMAN. Show your talents, show your animal reason.
Put human society to shame. Gentlemen, the animal you
see here with a tail behind and four hooves is a fellow of the
learned societies and a professor at our university where he
teaches the students riding and fighting. Now, use your
double reasoning; what do you do when you use your
double reasoning? Is there an ass in this learned gathering?

The horse shakes its head.

See the double reasoning, ladies and gentlemen. It's called
horse sense, this is no dumb animal, this is a person, a
human being. A brute of a man, and yet an animal, a beast,
une bête.

The horse behaves indecently.

That's it. Put society to shame. You see, the animal is still in
a state of nature, unidealised nature. Take a lesson from the
animal, ask the doctor, it can be dangerous to keep it in.
Man be natural, he says. You are created of dust, sand and
filth. Do you want to be more than dust, sand and filth? See
what reasoning! This creature can count even though it
can't use its fingers. Why? It can't just express itself and

make itself understood, it's a person metamorphosised. Tell the ladies and gentlemen what the time is. Which of the ladies and gentlemen has a watch?

SERGEANT. A watch? There, sir.

With a grandiose, deliberate gesture, he takes out a watch from his pocket.

MARIE. I must see this.

She climbs up on to the front bench. The SERGEANT *helps her.*

DRUM MAJOR. What a woman!

5.

MARIE's *room.*

MARIE *sits with the* CHILD *in her lap, and holds a little mirror in her hand.*

MARIE. That other one gave him his orders and he had to go.

She looks at her reflection.

How they glitter. What kind did he say they were? Sleep now, my boy, close your eyes hard.

The CHILD *holds his hands in front of his eyes.*

Tighter, that's it – quick now, otherwise he'll come and get you.

> (*Sings.*) If you don't close the window tight
> The gypsy boy will come at night
> And he will take you by the hand
> And lead you off to gypsy land.

She looks at her reflection again.

It's definitely gold. What will they look like when I dance, I wonder. Our kind have only this one corner in the whole world and a little bit of broken mirror, and yet my lips are as red as any madam's with her mirrors from floor to ceiling and fine gentlemen to kiss her hand. And I'm just a poor girl.

The child sits up.

Quiet now, boy, and close those eyes. Look at the sandman running across the wall. Close your eyes, if he looks into your eyes you'll go blind.

She makes light reflections with the mirror.

WOYZECK *comes in behind her. She puts her hands up over her ears.*

WOYZECK. What have you got there?

MARIE. Nothing.

WOYZECK. It's shining between your fingers.

MARIE. An earring. I found it.

WOYZECK. I've never found anything and you've found two at once.

MARIE. Aren't I clever?

WOYZECK. It's all right, Marie. How the child sleeps. Lift up his arm, the chair's pinching him. There are beads of sweat on his forehead. Nothing but work under the sun. We even sweat in our sleep. We poor folk. Here's more money, Marie: my pay and something from the Captain.

MARIE. God reward you, Franz.

WOYZECK. I've got to go! This evening, Marie.

He goes.

MARIE (*alone, after a pause*). Aren't I a bad girl? I could stab myself. What a world. We're all going to Hell, man and woman.

6.

At the CAPTAIN's.

The CAPTAIN *in a chair,* WOYZECK *shaving him.*

CAPTAIN. Slowly, Woyzeck, slowly, one thing at a time. You're making me dizzy. What am I going to do with the extra ten minutes you save? Imagine, Woyzeck, you've got a good thirty years yet to live, thirty years! That's 360 months. And days, hours, minutes. What are you going to do with all that time? Pace yourself, Woyzeck.

WOYZECK. Yes, Captain.

CAPTAIN. I worry about the world when I think of eternity. Keep busy, Woyzeck, keep busy. That's forever, forever! You can see that, can't you? And then again it's not eternity but just a passing moment, yes, a passing moment, Woyzeck. I shiver when I think that the world spins all the way round in one day! But what a waste of time! And where will it all end? I only have to look at a millwheel and I become melancholy.

WOYZECK. Yes, Captain.

CAPTAIN. Woyzeck, you look so hunted. A decent man doesn't, a decent man with a good clear conscience . . . Say something then, Woyzeck! What kind of weather it is today?

WOYZECK. Bad sir, windy.

CAPTAIN. I can feel it. There's such a rush out there! The wind has the same effect upon me as a mouse has. (*Craftily.*) I suppose it's a South-Northerly?

WOYZECK. Yes, Captain.

CAPTAIN. Hahaha. South-Northerly! Oh, you're so stupid, so horribly stupid. (*Moved.*) Woyzeck, you're a decent man – but (*Solemnly.*) you've no morals. Morals, that's when a person is moral, you understand me? It's a good word. You have a child without the blessing of the church, as our Right Reverend Garrison Preacher said, without the church's blessing. It wasn't me who said it.

WOYZECK. Captain Sir, our beloved Lord won't think any better of the little worm just because Amen was said over him before he was made. The Lord said, 'suffer the little children to come unto me'.

CAPTAIN. What did you say? What kind of strange answer is that? He makes me quite confused with his answers. I don't mean He, I mean you.

WOYZECK. We poor folk – you see, Captain, it's money, money, when you've got none. You can't set a fellow like me in the world on just morals, a man is flesh and blood as well. The likes of us are unblessed in this world and in the next. I expect when we get to Heaven we'll have to help out with the thunder.

CAPTAIN. Woyzeck, you have no virtue. You are not a virtuous man. Flesh and blood? When I'm lying by the window and it's been raining and I see the white stockings tripping down the alleyways – damn it, Woyzeck, I feel love! I too am flesh and blood. But Woyzeck, Virtue, Virtue! How am I supposed to spend my time? But I say to myself 'You are a virtuous man,' (*Moved.*) 'a decent man, a decent man.'

WOYZECK. Yes Captain, Virtue – I don't have that problem.
We ordinary people don't have any virtue, we just follow
our natures. But if I was a gentleman and had a hat and a
watch and a long overcoat and could talk nicely then I'd like
to be virtuous. It must be nice to have virtue, Captain, but
I'm a poor man.

CAPTAIN. Good Woyzeck, you're a decent man, a decent
man. But you think too much. It wears you down. You look
so hunted. Our discussion has quite upset me. Go now and
don't run so. Slowly, nice and slowly down the road.

7.

MARIE's *bedroom*.

MARIE, DRUM MAJOR.

DRUM MAJOR. Marie!

MARIE (*looking at him meaningfully*). Walk a few steps. Chest like a bull, beard like a lion. I'm the proudest woman alive.

DRUM MAJOR. On Sundays when I've got my big feathered helmet on and my white gloves – my God! Sometimes the prince says 'Christ! What a man!'

MARIE (*mocking*). Does he? (*Going to stand in front of him.*) Really?

DRUM MAJOR. And you're a Hell of a woman. By God, we'll set up a stud farm for drum majors, eh?

He takes her in his arms.

MARIE (*firmly*). Let go of me!

DRUM MAJOR. Wild animal!

MARIE (*violently*). Don't touch me!

DRUM MAJOR. You've got the Devil in your eyes!

MARIE. Oh who cares! It's all the same.

8.

MARIE's *room.*

MARIE, WOYZECK. WOYZECK *is staring at her and shaking his head.*

WOYZECK. H'm. Don't see anything. You should be able to see it, you should be able to hold it in your hands.

MARIE (*worried*). What is it, Franz? You're raving. Franz.

WOYZECK. A sin, such a big fat sin – it stinks so much you could smoke out all the angels from Heaven with it. You've got a red mouth Marie. No blisters? God, Marie, you're as beautiful as sin. Can mortal sin be so beautiful?

MARIE. Franz, you're delirious.

WOYZECK. Devil! Did he stand here? Like this? Like this?

MARIE. Well, since the day is long and the world is old, many people can have stood in the same place, one after another.

WOYZECK. I saw him.

MARIE. People see plenty if they've got two eyes and are not blind and the sun's shining.

WOYZECK. Whore!

MARIE. Don't touch me, Franz. Rather a knife in my body than your hand on mine. Even my father didn't dare touch me when I looked him in the eye, not since I was ten years old.

WOYZECK. Woman! No, there has to be something about you. Everyone is an abyss. You get dizzy when you look down. Maybe. She walks like innocence. Well, Innocence, you have a mark on you. Do I know? Do I know? Who knows?

He goes.

9.

At the DOCTOR's.

WOYZECK, *the* DOCTOR.

DOCTOR. What does this mean? A man of his word!

WOYZECK. What is it, Doctor?

DOCTOR. I saw you, Woyzeck, you pissed in the street, pissed against the wall like a dog. And three groschen a day plus food. Woyzeck, it's bad, the world is going bad, very bad.

WOYZECK. But Doctor, when nature calls . . .

DOCTOR. Nature calls, nature calls! Nature! Haven't I proved that the *musculus constrictor vesicae* is subject to the will? Nature! Woyzeck, man is free. In man, Nature manifests itself as freedom. Couldn't hold his urine!

He shakes his head, puts his hands behind his back and paces up and down.

Have you eaten your peas, Woyzeck? Nothing but peas, *cruciferae*, remember that. There's going to be a revolution in science, I'm going to blow it all to pieces. Uric acid nought point ten, ammonium hydrochlorate, hyperoxide. Woyzeck, don't you need another piss? Go in and try.

WOYZECK. I can't, Doctor.

DOCTOR (*emotionally*). But to piss against the wall! I have your written agreement in my hand. I saw it with my own eyes. I had just stuck my nose out of the window to let the rays of the sun fall on it in order to make some observations about sneezing.

He goes up close.

No, Woyzeck, I'm not getting angry. Angry is unhealthy. It's unscientific. I'm calm, quite calm. My pulse is its usual 60 and I tell you with the utmost coolness . . . God forbid that we should get angry over a mere human being, a human being. Now, if it had been a proteus . . . But really, you shouldn't have pissed against the wall.

WOYZECK. You see, Doctor, sometimes one is of a certain character, a structure. But with nature . . . it's a kind of a . . . what shall I say . . . ?

[*He clicks his fingers.*]

DOCTOR. Woyzeck, you're philosophising again.

WOYZECK (*confidentially*). Doctor, have you ever seen double nature? When the sun is at its highest point in the sky and it is as if the whole world is on fire – that's when a terrible voice spoke to me.

DOCTOR. Woyzeck, you have an *aberratio*.

WOYZECK (*putting his finger by his nose*). It's in the mushrooms, Doctor, that's where it is. Have you seen how they grow in patterns on the ground? If a man could only interpret them.

DOCTOR. Woyzeck, you have the finest *aberratio mentalis partialis* of the second category, quite pronounced. Woyzeck, I'm going to give you a rise. Second category: fixed idea but otherwise rational. Apart from that, going on as usual? Shaving the Captain?

WOYZECK. Yes, Doctor.

DOCTOR. Eating your peas?

WOYZECK. Every single one, Doctor! Give my wife the money for housekeeping . . .

DOCTOR. Carrying out your duties?

WOYZECK. Yes, sir.

DOCTOR. You're an interesting case, Woyzeck. You'll get a rise. Just keep it up. Let me feel your pulse. Yes.

10.

Street.

CAPTAIN, DOCTOR. *The* CAPTAIN *comes panting down the street [after the* DOCTOR. *He] stops, pants, looks about him.*

CAPTAIN. Doctor! Don't run about so, stop rowing along like that with your walking stick. You're racing towards death. A decent man with a clear conscience doesn't rush about like that, a decent man . . .

He grabs the DOCTOR *by the coat.*

Permit me to save a human life.

DOCTOR. I'm in a hurry, Captain, I'm in a hurry.

CAPTAIN. Doctor, I'm so melancholy, I have such melancholia. If I see my coat hanging on the wall I burst into tears.

DOCTOR. Hm, you're bloated, fat, thick neck. Apoplectic constitution. Yes, Captain, you're heading for *apoplexia cerebri*. You could get it just down one side and be half paralysed, or, if you're lucky, it will only affect the brain and you will merely vegetate away; those are your prospects for the next four weeks. Also I can assure you you'll make one of the most interesting cases and if the Good Lord wills it and your tongue is partially paralysed, then we'll make immortal experiments.

CAPTAIN. Doctor you mustn't scare me. It does happen that people die of pure fright. I can already envisage the mourners with lemons in their hands, but they'll say I was a decent man, a decent man . . . You coffin nail!

DOCTOR (*holding out his hat*). What is this, Captain? It's an empty headpiece, honoured square basher.

CAPTAIN (*making a dent in the hat*). And that is a dent in your hat, Doctor, hahaha. No offence meant, I'm a decent fellow but I can give as good as I get if I want to, Doctor, hahaha, if I want to!

WOYZECK *comes, tries to hurry past.*

What are you hurrying past for? Stop a bit, Woyzeck. He runs through the world like an open razor, you could cut yourself on him. He rushes about as if he had a regiment of castrates to shave, and would be hanged on account of the longest hair he missed before he could make his getaway. But *à propos* long beards, what was it I was going to say, Woyzeck? Long beards . . .

DOCTOR. A long beard under the chin, even Plinius says soldiers have to be weaned away from such things.

CAPTAIN (*continuing*). Yes, *à propos* long beards, Woyzeck, have you found any hairs from someone's beard in your soup recently? You know what I mean – a human hair, from the beard of a sapper, a sergeant or a drum major? Well, Woyzeck? But he's got an honest wife. Such things don't happen to him, of course.

WOYZECK. Yes, sir. What do you mean, sir?

CAPTAIN. Look at the expression on his face! . . . Not so much in your soup as when if you might pop around the corner you might find one on a pair of lips. Woyzeck, I have also felt love. The man's as white as chalk!

WOYZECK. Captain, I'm only a poor devil, I have nothing else in this world. Captain, if you're joking with me.

CAPTAIN. Joking? Me joke with you?

DOCTOR. Your pulse, Woyzeck, your pulse – short, violent, jumping, irregular.

WOYZECK. Captain, the Earth is as hot as Hell. I'm cold, ice cold. Hell is cold, I'd bet on it. Bitch, bitch, impossible.

CAPTAIN. Do you want a couple of bullets in your head? He's stabbing me with his eyes. I'm only telling you for your own good. Because you're a decent fellow, Woyzeck, a decent fellow.

DOCTOR. Face muscles are rigid, tense, occasionally twitching. Behaviour: excited, tense.

WOYZECK. I'm going. It's possible. The bitch. It's very possible. Nice weather we're having, Captain. See what a beautiful solid grey sky, makes you want to knock a nail in and hang yourself. All for the difference between yes and no. Is the 'no' to blame for the 'yes' or the 'yes' to blame for the 'no'? I must think about that.

He goes out, with long steps, first slowly and then quickly.

DOCTOR (*rushing after him*). A phenomenon! Hey, Woyzeck! A rise!

CAPTAIN. That fellow makes me dizzy. How fast the big rascal runs, groping like a spider's shadow, and the little one runs after. The big one is the thunder and the little one is the lightning. Haha! Grotesque, grotesque!

11.

The Guardroom.

WOYZECK, ANDRES.

ANDRES. The landlady she has a maid
              Sits night and day amongst the herbs,
              Sitting by her garden fence –

WOYZECK. Andres.

ANDRES. What?

WOYZECK. Nice weather.

ANDRES. Sunday weather. Music outside town, the women
    are on their way. The people are steaming. I like it.

WOYZECK (*restless*). Dancing. Andres, they're dancing.

ANDRES. At the Horse and Star.

WOYZECK. Dance, dance!

ANDRES. What does it matter?

              Sitting by her garden fence
              All day and night just to observe
              The passing of two regiments –

WOYZECK. Andres, I have no peace.

ANDRES. Idiot.

WOYZECK. I must go out. My head is swimming. Dancing,
    dancing, dancing. Will she have hot hands? Damn it,
    Andres!

ANDRES. What do you want?

WOYZECK. I must go quickly, I must see.

ANDRES. You slave. Just because of her.

WOYZECK. I must go out! It's so hot in here!

12.

An inn. Open windows, dancing. Benches outside.

JOURNEYMEN, DRINKERS, DANCERS, WOYZECK.

FIRST JOURNEYMAN.
> I have a shirt that isn't mine.
> My soul it stinks of brandywine.

SECOND JOURNEYMAN. Shall I punch a hole in your face out of friendship, brother? As one friend to another, come on, I'll punch a hole in your face. I'm a man too, you know – I'll knock the fleas out of him.

FIRST JOURNEYMAN. My soul, my soul it stinks of brandywine! Even money rots, Forget-me-not. How beautiful the world is. I could weep a waterbutt full of tears from melancholy. I wish our noses were a pair of bottles and we could pour them down each other's throats.

OTHERS (*in a chorus*).
> A hunter came riding through the snow
> With a bag of hares and a brace of geese,
> Singing his way across the heath,
> The sky above and the earth beneath.
> > A-hunting we will go.

WOYZECK *goes and stands by the window.* MARIE *and the* DRUM MAJOR *dance by. They don't see him.*

WOYZECK. Him! Her! Damn!

MARIE. On and on and on and on . . . !

WOYZECK (*choking*). On and on, on and on.

He starts up, sinks back on the bench.

On and on, on and on.

He claps his hands.

Keep spinning, keep turning. Why doesn't God snuff out
the sun so they can all fall on top of each other in their
fornication? Man and woman, man and beast, in broad
daylight, on the backs of your hands like flies. Woman!
She's hot! On and on, on and on! Look at him grabbing
her, her body. He's got her like I had her in the beginning.

He sinks dazed to the floor. The FIRST JOURNEYMAN *makes
a speech from the table top.*

FIRST JOURNEYMAN. Yes, it sometimes happens that
the wanderer who stands leaning against the stream of
time challenges divine wisdom and asks himself, 'Why
does Man exist?' 'Why does Man exist?' But verily I say
unto you – what would the farmer or the cooper, the
shoemaker or the doctor live by if God had not made
Man? How would the tailor get his living if God had not
planted the sense of shame in Man's breast? And how
would the soldier live if God had not armed him with the
desire to be killed? Doubt not therefore – there is much
that is good and sweet, but all earthly joys are vanity. Even
money rots. So, in conclusion, brethren, let us piss on the
cross so a Jew will die.

During the general jubilation, WOYZECK *wakes up and rushes
away.*

13.

In a field.

WOYZECK. On and on, on and on – squeal and squeak go
  the fiddles and the pipes. On and on, on and on. Stop the
  music! Who's talking down there?

He puts his ear to the ground.

Eh? What do you say? Louder, louder! Stab? Stab the she
wolf dead. Stab, stab the she wolf dead. Shall I? Must I?
Do I hear it up there too? Is the wind saying it? I can hear
it on and on, on and on. Stab her dead, dead!

14.

A barrack room. Night.

ANDRES, WOYZECK, *in the same bed.*

WOYZECK [(*shaking him*)]. Andres!

ANDRES *mumbles in his sleep.*

Hey! Hey, Andres.

ANDRES. Well, what is it?

WOYZECK. I can't sleep. When I close my eyes everything just goes round and round, and I hear the fiddles. On and on, on and on. And it speaks out of the walls. Don't you hear anything?

ANDRES. Ah, let her dance. I'm tired. God keep us. Amen.

WOYZECK. It's saying 'Stab, stab!' It pierces me between the eyes like a knife.

ANDRES. Sleep, you idiot.

He goes back to sleep.

WOYZECK. On and on, on and on.

15.

DOCTOR's *courtyard.*

STUDENTS *and* WOYZECK *below,* DOCTOR *at the window.*

DOCTOR. Gentlemen, I find myself on the roof like David when he saw Bathsheba. But I don't see anything except the girls' knickers hanging on the line in the school yard. Gentlemen, we have reached the important question of the subject's relation to the object. Let us take a creature in which the divine's organic self-affirmation reaches one of its higher manifestations and examine its relationship to space, the earth, the universe. Gentlemen, if I throw this cat out of the window, how will this creature, in accordance with its instinct, maintain its centre of gravity? Hello there, Woyzeck . . . (*Bellowing.*)Woyzeck!

[WOYZECK *catches the cat.*]

WOYZECK. It's bitten me, Doctor!

DOCTOR. But lad! He holds the little wretch as if it were his grandmother.

He comes down.

WOYZECK. I've got the shakes, Doctor.

DOCTOR (*pleased*). Ah, ah, wonderful, Woyzeck!

He rubs his hands and takes the cat.

What we have here, gentlemen, a new species of rabbit-louse, a marvellous species . . .

He takes out a magnifying glass. The cat runs away.

Gentlemen, animals have no scientific instinct . . . But here is something else to observe. See this man here? For three months he's been eating nothing but peas. Observe the effects, just feel: what an irregular pulse! And his eyes!

WOYZECK. Doctor it's gone all black.

He sits.

DOCTOR. Courage, Woyzeck, just another couple of days and then it's finished. Feel him, gentlemen.

They feel his temples, pulse and chest.

While you're at it, wiggle your ears a bit for the gentlemen. I wanted to show you this, two small muscles he uses together. Off you go, Woyzeck.

WOYZECK. But Doctor . . .

DOCTOR. Do I have to wiggle your ears for you? You wretch! You want to follow the cat's example. That's it. Now, gentlemen, you see he's turning into a donkey. That's a consequence of being brought up by a female and using the mother tongue. How many strands of hair has your mother, out of pure fondness, plucked out for mementos? It's getting rather thin on top these past few days. Yes, peas, gentlemen.

16.

Inn.

DRUM MAJOR WOYZECK, DRINKERS.

DRUM MAJOR. I'm a man.

He beats his breast.

A man, I said. Who wants some, eh? Unless you're the Lord God Almighty and pissed as well, keep away from me – I'll stick your nose up your arse. I'll – (*To* WOYZECK.) Oi, you, drink! I wish the whole world were schnapps! Schnapps – a man has to drink.

WOYZECK *whistles.*

You . . . ! Shall I pull your tongue out of your throat and tie it around your neck?

They fight. WOYZECK *loses.*

I won't leave you enough breath for an old woman's fart.

WOYZECK *sits, exhausted and trembling, on a bench.*

Now you can whistle till you're blue in the face.

> Brandywine it is my love
> Brandywine gives you courage.

FIRST DRINKER. He's had enough.

SECOND DRINKER. He's bleeding.

WOYZECK. One thing after another.

17.

Barracks.

WOYZECK, ANDRES.

WOYZECK. Haven't you heard anything?

ANDRES. He's still in there with a friend.

WOYZECK. He said something.

ANDRES. How do you know? What shall I say? 'Well, he laughed and said what a tasty woman, great thighs and hot through!'

WOYZECK. So that's what he said. What was it I dreamed last night? Wasn't it about a knife? What idiotic dreams people have.

ANDRES. Where are you going, Franz?

WOYZECK. To fetch wine for my officer. But Andres – she was the only girl.

ANDRES. Who?

WOYZECK. Nothing. Adieu.

He goes.

18.

A small shop.

WOYZECK, JEW.

WOYZECK. The gun's too dear.

JEW. You buy it or you don't.

WOYZECK. What does the knife cost?

JEW. It's rather sharp. Are you going to cut your throat? Well, what's it to be? I'll give it to you as cheap as anyone else. You can get your death cheap – but not for nothing. What do you say? You'll have an economical death.

WOYZECK. That one can cut more than bread. . .

JEW. Two groschen.

WOYZECK. There.

He goes.

JEW. 'There.' As if it were nothing. And yet it's money. You dog.

19.

MARIE's *room.*

MARIE, CHILD, *the* IDIOT. *The* IDIOT *lies talking to himself while he counts on his fingers.* MARIE *is leafing through the Bible.*

IDIOT. If the king has got the gold crown . . . tomorrow I'll fetch the queen her child. Come on, sausage, said the black pudding.

MARIE. 'Nor was guile found in his mouth . . . ' Dear Lord, don't look at me.

She turns more pages.

'The scribes and the pharisees brought to him a woman taken in adultery and set her in the midst . . . and Jesus said unto her, "Neither do I condemn thee. Go, and sin no more."'

She clasps her hands together.

My God, my God I can't. Oh Lord just help me so that I can pray.

The CHILD *child nestles up to her.*

It breaks my heart to look at the child. (*To the* IDIOT.) You there, basking in the sun.

The IDIOT *takes the child and is quiet.*

Franz hasn't been here. Not today, not yesterday. No, it's getting too hot.

She opens the window and reads on.

'And stood at his feet weeping and began to wash his feet with her tears and wipe them with the hairs of her head and kissed his feet and anointed them with ointment.'

She beats her breast.

Everything is dead. Saviour, saviour! If only I could anoint your feet!

20.

Barracks.

ANDRES, WOYZECK *going through his possessions.*

WOYZECK. This waistcoat isn't general issue. You might have some use for it.

ANDRES (*stiffly*). Yes.

WOYZECK. This cross is my sister's, and the ring.

ANDRES. Yes.

WOYZECK. I have a picture of Jesus, two hearts and real gold. It was inside my mother's Bible, where it said,

> Lord, as you were red and sore
> So let my heart be evermore

My mother can't feel anything anymore, only when the sun shines on her hands – it won't matter.

ANDRES. Yes.

WOYZECK. Friedrich Johann Franz Woyzeck, rifleman, Four Company, Second Battalion, Second Regiment, born on the Feast of The Annunciation, 20th July. Today I am 30 years, seven months and twelve days old.

ANDRES. Franz, you'll end up in hospital. You need some schnapps with gunpowder in it. That'll kill your fever.

WOYZECK. Yes, Andres, when the carpenter sweeps up his shavings, no one knows whose head will be laid to rest on them.

21.

A street.

MARIE, GRANDMOTHER, MARGRET.

MARGRET.   The sun was shining on Candlemas day,
                 The corn was blue and yellow the hay.
                 They crossed to the meadow two by two,
                 The fiddler played a mournful song
                 And the girls had all red stockings on –

FIRST CHILD. That wasn't very nice.

SECOND CHILD. You're never satisfied.

FIRST CHILD. Marie, you sing something.

MARIE. I can't.

FIRST CHILD. Why not?

MARIE. Because.

SECOND CHILD. But why because?

THIRD CHILD. Tell us a story, Grandma.

GRANDMOTHER. All right. Once there was a poor child
  with no mother and no father. Everything was dead and
  there wasn't a soul left on Earth. Everything was dead and
  the child went out and searched day and night. But since
  there was no one left on Earth he wanted to go up to
  Heaven, and indeed the Moon looked down kindly at him,
  but when he got up to the Moon it was just a piece of rotten
  wood. So he set off for the Sun, and when he got there it
  was only a withered sunflower, and when he got to the stars
  they were only golden gnats that a shrike had stuck to a

blackthorn bush, and when the child wanted to go back down to Earth, it was just an upside-down chamber pot and the child was all alone. Then he sat down and cried and he's still sitting there to this day, all alone.

WOYZECK *comes.*

WOYZECK. Marie.

MARIE (*scared*). What is it?

WOYZECK. We're going now, Marie. It's time.

MARIE. Where?

WOYZECK. How do I know?

22.

In a wood by a pond.

MARIE, WOYZECK.

MARIE. That's the town over there. It's so gloomy.

WOYZECK. Stop here. Come and sit down.

MARIE. I have to go.

WOYZECK. You've no need to run your feet off.

MARIE. You're so strange.

WOYZECK. Do you know how long it's been, Marie?

MARIE. Two years come Whitsun.

WOYZECK. Do you know how long it's going to be as well?

MARIE. I have to go and make supper.

WOYZECK. Are you cold, Marie? And yet you're so warm. What hot lips you've got, hot. Hot whore's breath. And yet I'd give the kingdom of Heaven to kiss them again . . . Are you cold? When you're cold you won't feel cold anymore. The morning dew won't make you feel cold.

MARIE. What are you saying?

WOYZECK. Nothing.

MARIE. The moon's rising. So red.

WOYZECK. Like blood on iron.

MARIE. What are you going to do? You're so pale, Franz.

He raises his knife.

Franz! Stop! For the love of God help! Help!

WOYZECK *stabs wildly.*

WOYZECK. Take that, and that. You can't die? There! There! She's still twitching, not yet, not yet. Once more.

He stabs one last time.

Are you dead? Dead! Dead!

He lets the knife fall and runs away.

23.

The inn.

[JOURNEYMEN, DANCERS, DRINKERS, KÄTHE,
   WOYZECK, IDIOT.]

WOYZECK. Dance, everyone, on and on. Sweet and stink.
   He'll take you all in the end anyway.

> (*sings.*) Tell me why, my dear daughter,
> And what have you done?
> Gone off with a soldier
> And polished his gun –

I'm hot, Käthe. I'm hot. Hot! Hot!

He takes off his jacket.

The Devil takes the one and lets the other go. You're warm
too, Käthe. Why's that? But you'll be cold one day, even
you. Be nice now, Käthe. Couldn't you sing?

KÄTHE.   In Schwaben I am not at home
               And I don't wear long dresses,
               For finery and pointed shoes
               A servant girl should never choose –

WOYZECK. No, no shoes. You can get to Hell barefoot.

KÄTHE.   Ah, no, my friend that was ill said.
               Keep your money and keep your bed –

WOYZECK. Really, I don't want to get covered in blood.

KÄTHE. What's that on your hand?

WOYZECK. Me? Me?

KÄTHE. Red! Blood!

People gather round them.

WOYZECK. Blood? Blood?

DRINKER. Urgh! Blood!

WOYZECK. I think I cut myself on my (right) hand.

DRINKER. But how did it get onto your elbow?

WOYZECK. I wiped it off.

DRINKER. What? You wiped your right hand on your right elbow? That's clever.

IDIOT. And the giant said, 'Fe Fi Fo Fum, I smell the blood of an Englishman . . . '

WOYZECK. What the Hell do you want? What's it got to do with you? Out of my way! Or I'll . . . You think I've killed someone. Am I a murderer, eh? What are you staring at? Stare at yourselves. Out of the way!

He rushes out.

24.

By the pond.

WOYZECK *alone.*

WOYZECK. The knife, where's the knife? I put it down
somewhere. It will betray me. Closer and closer. What kind
of a place is this? What's that? Something moved. Quiet.
Somewhere just here. Marie. Ha. Marie. Still, completely
still. Why are you so pale, Marie? Why have you got a red
ribbon round your neck? Who have you earned that from
with your sins? You were black with sin, black. Was it me
made you so pale? What's your hair so wild for? Haven't
you got it in plaits today? . . . The knife, the knife. Have I
got it? Here!

He runs to the water.

There! Away with it!

He throws the knife into the pond.

It will sink like a stone in that dark water . . . No, it's too
near the beach where they swim.

He wades out into the water and throws the knife further out.

There! But in the summer when they dive after mussels?
Ach! It will rust anyway, who'd recognise it? If only I'd
destroyed it. Am I still bloody? I must wash. There's one
stain. And there's another.

He wades further out.

Appendix: Fragments

1. IDIOT (KARL), CHILD (CHRISTIAN), WOYZECK

KARL *has the* CHILD *in front of him on his lap.*

IDIOT. He's fallen in the water, he's fallen in the water, he's fallen in the water!

WOYZECK. Rascal Christian.

IDIOT (*a fixed stare*). He's fallen in the water.

   WOYZECK *tries to caress the child but it struggles free and screams.*

WOYZECK. My God!

IDIOT. He's fallen in the water.

WOYZECK. Christian, I'll get you a hobby-horse, sa, sa.

   The CHILD *resists.*

   (*To* KARL.) He's going to buy the rascal a hobby-horse.

   KARL *stares ahead fixedly.*

   Jump horse jump!

KARL (*joyfully*). Jump horse, jump horse!

   He runs away with the CHILD.

2. TWO JOURNEYMEN.

FIRST JOURNEYMAN. Stop!

SECOND JOURNEYMAN. Hear that? Quiet! There!

FIRST JOURNEYMAN. Ooh! There! What a sound!

SECOND JOURNEYMAN. It's the water. It's calling out. It's ages since anyone was drowned. Let's go. It's not good to hear this.

FIRST JOURNEYMAN. Ooh! There it is again. As if someone was dying.

SECOND JOURNEYMAN. It's uncanny. So dark, all foggy and grey and the buzz of the beetles like cracked bells. Let's go!

FIRST JOURNEYMAN. No. So clear, so loud. Up there. Come on!

3. *Street.* CHILDREN

FIRST CHILD. Come on Mariechen!

SECOND CHILD. What?

FIRST CHILD. Didn't you know? Everyone's gone already. There's a woman lying out there!

SECOND CHILD. Where?

FIRST CHILD. On the left above the earthworks in the little woods by the red cross.

SECOND CHILD. Come on or we'll miss it. They'll carry it away.

4. CORONER, JUDGE, DOCTOR, BARBER

CORONER. A decent murder, a real murder, a lovely murder, as lovely as you could wish for. We haven't had one like this for so long!